ETHICS AND ECONOMICS

The Lord Acton Essay Competition Series

Ethics and Economics

Graduate Essays on the Moral Foundation of Political Economy

Introduction by James V. Schall, S. J.

Acton Institute • Grand Rapids, Michigan
1998

ISBN: 1-880595-14-1

Acton Institute for the Study of Religion and Liberty
161 Ottawa Northwest, Suite 301
Grand Rapids, Michigan, 49503
Telephone: (616) 454-3080 • Facsimile: (616) 454-9454

Cover Design and Typesetting by LaGrand Ink

Printed in the United States of America

Contents

v

Foreword

Rev. Robert A. Sirico
President, Acton Institute

The Acton Institute was founded in 1990 to help promote a free society characterized by individual liberty and sustained by religious principles. In the past nine years we have worked to advance freedom and promote virtue by providing resources for the religious leaders of today and educating those of tomorrow. One of the first ways we sought to encourage young religious intellectuals to consider the importance of sound economic thinking in relation to moral and religious concerns, and one of the Acton Institute's first programs, was the Lord Acton Essay Competition.

For this writing competition, we select a quotation from the Institute's namesake – Lord John Emerich Edward Dalberg Acton – and ask seminarians and religious studies students, as well as students with a demonstrated interest in religious issues, to reflect upon themes encapsulated by that quotation. The following quotation was chosen for the 1998 contest:

> The moral foundation of political economy is not the satisfaction of appetite but the fulfillment of duties. Labour, patience, justice, peace, and self-denial are the mainsprings of economical production, and the metaphysical basis of the science is not in a philosophy which reduces religion and science to mere satisfaction of an appetite, like eating or drinking, but in the verification of the promise, "Seek ye first the kingdom of God and His justice and all these things" – the necessaries of life – "shall be added unto you."

This passage addresses the interplay of morality, individual freedom, and economic activity – an area of study vital to the Institute. In fact it is the study of the "moral foundation of political economy" that the Institute encourages through programs like this essay competition.

We vigorously promoted the 1998 competition to every seminary and religious studies program in the United States and Canada, as well as select colleges and seminaries throughout the world. From the large volume of applicants representing a variety of religious traditions, we selected ten finalists. Those ten essays were then sent out to a panel of distinguished judges, who ranked them according to their scholarly content and literary style. After we compiled the comments of the judges, we selected a first, second, and third place winner, and two honorable mentions. It is these essays you now hold in your hands.

I want to thank all who applied, our panel of judges, and most especially, the friends and supporters of the Acton Institute for making the 1998 Lord Acton Essay Contest such a success. It is in this way, by equipping the next generation of religious leaders with the tools of sound economic thinking and stimulating their thought, that we will help promote a society that is both free and virtuous.

Introduction:
Justice, Pleasure, Right, Duty, and Beyond

James V. Schall, S. J.
Georgetown University

> We know how to provide *enough* and do not require any violent, inhuman, aggressive technologies to do so. There is no economic problem and, in a sense, there never has been. But there is a moral problem and moral problems are not . . . capable of being solved so that future generations can live without effort.
>
> —E. F. Schumacher[1]

I.

Bernard de Mandeville (1670–1733), famously or infamously, suggested that the cause of wealth is vice. It is a provocative view, no doubt. If everyone were perfect and subdued, he thought, no one would demand anything. Everyone would be content with little. With no aggregate demand, there would be no incentive for production. With no demand and production, no exchange and increase of wealth would be possible. Thus, if we will not drink beer, there will be no brewing industry. No brewing industry will mean no growing of hops and barley, thus no farmers, no market for bottles or cans, no Clydesdales, nor anything refreshing to drink at baseball games.

By contrast, Plato himself had indicated, through Glaucon in *The Republic*, that a society driven by unlimited and ever more sophisticated demands would simply be a "city of pigs." It would be a people with no interest higher than producing ever more sophisticated items for consumption. Such a people, without military guardians, would be unable to defend themselves from their own passions or from the desires of other cities coveting what they had produced for their luxury.

In another variant of this theme, Hegel was later to suggest that virtuous societies have no history; nothing occurs except a repetition of rather boring events associated with ordinary life. In some sense, then, economics has been saddled with a rather dubious heritage. Growth will be caused by vice and distribution by greed, while virtue will produce stagnation.

For example, certain governments, because their own people lack internal virtue, desperately buy out the poppy supply of other countries that sell drugs in order not to ruin the "legitimate" business of the enterprising farmers in a poor country who grow the flowers for profit. In this case vice seems to promote economic growth.

On the other hand, we have seen that selling surplus farm products at a low price (or giving items away outright) in a foreign market for humanitarian purposes often ruins the higher-priced production of local farmers. This ruins an industry needed for self-sustaining growth. Doing good seems to foster further wrong. Clearly, the connection between vice and growth needs to be addressed. Is there, in other words, a case for virtue and growth? This is the import of the insightful essays presented here.

One major interpretation of the Industrial Revolution and its ongoing consequences suggests that the market mechanism that enabled such widespread wealth to be produced in the first place ended up impoverishing the masses. This is the basis of classic socialist rhetoric. The fact is, however, that Marx's taunt that over the years the rich are getting richer and the poor poorer is not true. Rather, what has happened is that everyone is getting richer at differing rates – provided he enters the market with a knowledge of how it operates and a will to work it. "Exploitation" is not an adequate explanation of poverty. The theory of exploitation itself impedes growth as it misunderstands the requirements of growth.

This long-range economic growth does not deny that wars and rumors of war will happen, though it does question that economics is the main cause. Neither does it doubt that many individuals, whether by accident or by their own choices, will fall by the wayside. The need for something beyond justice will always remain. The fact is, however, that for three centuries the world has seen a sustained growth of wealth and population that suggests that the problems of historic poverty can and are being solved if only we apply the proper means to them.

As the world has become richer at differing rates and in differing circumstances, the possibility of using this wealth wrongly has increased. Freedom means that there is no way to guarantee that wealth will be used properly unless those who produce and use it choose to act virtuously. The moral dilemma does not lie in the wealth itself but in the souls of those who produce and distribute it and in the habits of those who need it and use it.

A well-ordered government can contribute to the proper development and use of wealth. It should be noted, however, that said contribution is by no means guaranteed and is always limited. Indeed, the overall record of governments on this score has not been encouraging. The main source for correcting any imbalances in the human condition (which will find, in turn, that some imbalances in goods are natural), will not come from the government. Certainly, the abuse of governmental power has been the cause of the greatest slaughters of the bloody twentieth century. This slaughter, like wide-spread poverty itself, has been caused, more than by anything else, by faulty economic ideas chosen by ideological governments. There should be no doubt of this fact, although I do not deny the positive good that governments ought to, and can, encourage.

We can thus continue these reflections with several basic propositions: 1) The rich are not rich because the poor are poor; in the beginning, all were poor. 2) The ultimate cause of wealth is not land, resources, or even labor, but rather the human brain, itself ordained to know *what is*. 3) The poor are capable of becoming rich, particularly by learning from those who have grasped how not to be poor. 4) Not every proposal for moving from poverty to prosperity is successful. 5) The purpose of political economy is not that the citizens, whether poor or rich, be "taken care of" by someone else; instead, each should provide for his own life by virtue of his own enterprise, work, and sacrifice in a fair system of exchange. 6) Governments primarily exist not to grant well-being to the populace, but to provide stability and justice. 7) Freedom allows for the implementation of new and improved courses of action; it also means that men may choose to do evil. They distort the workings of justice and brotherhood. 8) A relatively poor society can be a virtuous one; a relatively rich one can be permeated with vice, and vice versa.

II.

Plato was concerned with the potential philosophers, with those not unlike the young men who have authored the essays which follow. Plato devoted himself particularly to those potential philosophers whose souls ought to be open to the highest things, but whose internal lack of discipline or unguided desire could easily deflect them from *what is*, from what is important. It has long been both popularly assumed and philosophically affirmed, contrary to both Plato and Aristotle, that those who devoted themselves to the highest things were, by that very fact, neglecting the "human things," the "things of this world," particularly the things of man's "estate."

Each of these essays intimates in its own way, following Lord Acton's recollection of Matthew's "Seek ye first the kingdom of God," that a prosperous political economy will either operate improperly or cease to exist altogether if the production and workings of the economy itself are seen to be the first and only purpose of human living. Indeed, as modernity continues, we begin to see that the myth of a prosperous economy can be pictured as an alternative to God, particularly as the commandments and principles of virtue are presented not as the way to human well-being, but as its primary impediment. Morality is accused of being an impediment to prosperity.

Lord Acton's statement, on which these essays are formulated, contrasts "appetite" and "duty." He even seems to intimate that "eating and drinking" are "mere satisfaction of appetite." Eating and drinking, however, are not "mere" satisfactions of appetite. They are the means by which we continue to live within the order of nature that exists within each being. Appetite as such is part of our natural endowment; each appetite has a purpose. The pleasure that follows the exercise of our desires for our proper goods is not an evil or a disorder, as Aristotle and Aquinas remind us. Eating and drinking are enjoyable even if we must do them in order to be, which is their primary function. Indeed, making it possible to eat and drink in safety, abundance, and comfort is one of the primary purposes of any economy and the proud boast of modern productive society.

"Duty," moreover, is not something by itself, for its own sake, in some Kantian sense. If we have a "duty," it is because of what we are. All of our proper activities have their proper pleasures and purposes. These pleasures and purposes can be the occasion of our misusing them, but we should not think that the fact that we have appetite or pleasure is somehow a sign that something is wrong with us. These are our "inclinations," as Aquinas calls them, and indicate, when we think on them properly, what is right with us. They indicate the kind of beings we are: mortal beings composed of body and soul. What we are is directed to what is beyond or more than ourselves. This is why Aristotle told us not to listen to those who tell us merely to attend to "human" and not also to divine things, why Christ told us to seek first the kingdom of God.

III.

"The moral foundation of political economy," to use Acton's phrase, rests on the connection of liberty with right, of right with duty, of duty with leisure and delight, and of all with transcendence. At the beginning of this essay, I cited a surprising passage from the well-known British economist, E. F. Schumacher, in which he reminds us that our "economic" problems are not really economic, but moral in nature; they are problems that cannot be simply passed on from generation to generation. They need to be chosen and internalized by each person in each generation at the risk of deflecting material goods from their proper purposes. Likewise, work itself is not something done exclusively for its own sake. Rather, work – while being an expression of human dignity and concrete accomplishment – aims at a product, aims at the material well-being in which something more than work can happen. The basis of culture, as Josef Pieper wrote in a famous thesis, is not work, but leisure: what lies beyond work.

Several of the writers in this volume mention the attention that Pope John Paul II has given to the notion of work and the primacy of the worker with his needs and those of his family over some impersonal economic system. Yet, the need of work implies a system in which work is both normal and possible. The purpose of work is not simply work. The fact that we have creative powers within our nature indicates that we ought to work in and improve the world, not only to make it minimally provide for us, but also to make things elegant and noble. The world is not a parsimonious place, in spite of the dogmas of the ecologists.

When Aristotle talked of "commutative" justice, he indicated that its immediate object fell into two general areas. The first had to do with restoring the damages that we do to others by accident or deliberate fault. The second, the one that is important here, is the fact that this form of justice enables us to enter into agreements, into binding promises, whereby, as Acton said, we can organize the future and cause something worthwhile to come into being and, in so doing, gain our livelihood. The "common good," as a context for just relationships, recognizes that an abundance of good things is possible if we keep our contracts and if we permit, organize and encourage everyone to bring forth and offer his talents to others.

Work, genius, and ordinary endeavor ought to be available to others in an exchange whereby everyone does not do the same thing. Each person in the economy ought to be able to reflect that what he does is in some significant way actually worthwhile for human good taken in its broadest sense. Sean Mattie observes, in this regard, that "conventional economics would surely welcome the practical consequence of this Christian teaching – a system of steady production and equitable exchange." A principal reason for the malfunctioning or non-functioning of economies in which the well-being of a people is at stake is precisely the lack of moral, not technical, criteria whereby these desired results are obtained. The famous "option for the poor" is largely a question of choosing the right system that will enable the poor themselves to become "not poor."

Schumacher also intimates that the reason the poor are poor – the alleviation of which is the great external cause of our time and almost the only remaining acknowledged moral cause – is not because of a lack of knowledge. Rather, poverty in the twentieth century is largely the result of poor or erroneous choices by political and civil leaders, together with the free or forced consent of their populace, about how

to attain their own economic good. These choices are further compli-
cated by improper ideas concerning the relation of government to this
purpose.

Likewise, poverty may also be the result not of ignorance about
what can be done, but of refusing to embrace the discipline and the
ethic whereby what is known can actually be made malignant. As
Joshua Hochschild writes, "Acton perceived in Smith's economic
observations not the assumption of selfishness and vice, but an affirmation of the central importance of discipline and virtue." Yet discipline and virtue are not solely ends in themselves. They are, in turn,
oriented to what is beyond them, to what is no longer economic or
political. While it is permissible to speak of duty and virtue as goods in
and of themselves, they are also, as they are achieved by work and
exchange, used in pursuit of further duty and virtue. Only when a sufficiency of material goods is in place do the higher purposes of human
living begin to come into focus. Ironically, a society that is not attuned
to these higher things eventually risks even its material well-being, for
it misunderstands the purposes of the virtues that sustain it.

IV.

Zachary Calo remarks that "liberty cannot be based on the satisfaction of individual appetites. The benefits and privileges that freedom creates are wholly dependent on meeting the obligations and
sacrifices that freedom requires." Calo touches here upon what might
be called the paradox of freedom. Aristotle had observed that the char-
acteristic end or purpose of the Greek form of "democracy," itself a
bad form or regime, was precisely a "freedom" presupposed to no purpose. In fact, this freedom referred to an order of soul in the populace
in which there was no order; freedom meant precisely the denial of
order. Whatever was chosen was all right as there was no principle of
distinction among choices; anything one chose to do was perfectly
acceptable.

In Athens, as we learn from the case of Socrates, the free people
could not tell any difference between a fool and a philosopher.
Freedom meant doing whatever one chose; no way of life was better
than another. No doubt this understanding of democracy is being ever

more frequently practiced in our modern states as well, as we come to find a dogmatic refusal to connect liberty with any object. In fact, many deny the existence of such a connection. Acton, on the other hand, couples freedom with doing what we ought in a world where an objective good exists and is knowable.

"The things of this world are meant to be a tool to advance mankind," Michael Black writes, "and if the 'self' in self-government is unvirtuous, there is no reason to expect that the government linked to it will be any different." We live in a time in which the separation of private from public life is said to be absolute, that nothing can be concluded about the performance of a person in public life from his private life, either virtuous or unvirtuous. Black calls our attention to an earlier tradition, to the Platonic idea that all regimes are reflective of the souls of those who compose them, not only the souls of the leaders, but also the souls of those who are responsible for electing and sustaining those leaders. Without attention to lack of virtue, the souls of the leaders and the souls of the citizens come to approximate each other. Thus, leaders and citizens can corrupt each other.

V.

"Duty to God and duty to fellow humans, the essence of the 'two tables' of the decalogue, provide the foundation for a civil society. In seeking first the kingdom of God and His righteousness," Jonathan Barlow explains, "we escape both prideful, Nietzschean individualism and soul-killing collectivism. By providing a source of ethical verification which transcends the state itself, religious ethics destroy any kind of 'might makes right' claim on the part of magistrates." Barlow touches on two fundamental points here. The first inquires whether the magistrates have become an absolute law unto themselves so that no higher appeal exists other than their fluctuating opinions. The second is whether what is "beyond" the state is not required at least in principle for any real alternative to the absolute primacy of the magistrates and the state.

Modern civil societies are founded, some say, on "rights" and "values." Both of these words have dubious origins in modern philosophy and must be treated gingerly. Many from classical and religious backgrounds are wont to see in these words, as they do in the word "duties," no problem. But a certain precision must be acknowledged before their use can be promoted. "Rights" today generally mean "will-rights," assertions stemming typically from Hobbes that have no objective grounding other than desire. "Values" come from Max Weber and again mean anything we want them to mean. "Values" are precisely rooted in the inability to know any objective order or good. Thus, as do "will-rights," they presuppose a skepticism about the good. The word "duty," which ought to mean the objective proper good in a relationship, is more defensible than the word "right," and still has Kantian overtones. It has a kind of bare obligation connected to it that is not rooted in objective being and, in this way, joins the modern usage of the words "right" and "value."

All of these essays have endeavored to re-establish the fact that something exists that is worth doing. They have endeavored to escape from any skepticism about the good that would place its origin solely in what we do personally and socially, simply in whatever we want, no matter what that want might be. When Acton attacked the separation of desire and duty in the nineteenth century, he did not intend to suggest that desire had no ontological basis. Rather, he proposed to return desire to its proper function as a power directed toward what was worthy and good.

Acton, however, along with these writers whom he has influenced, was quite aware that we should see in duty not just something we "must" do, but something also worth doing simply because it is good. He realized that the highest human purposes for which all the orders of economics and politics exist still need to be consciously recognized. The kingdom of God, as Augustine taught us, is the end of our being. Without it, we will spend our lives in a futile search for it. The tragedy of our times is not that we have denied the existence of the City of God, but rather that we have sought to locate it where it is not. These essays serve to point us back in the right direction, to the purpose of the economy in its relation to the polity, and to the purpose of the polity in its relation to the transcendent purpose of man in this world and beyond.

Notes

1. E. F. Schumacher, *A Guide for the Perplexed* (New York: Harper Colophon, 1977), 140.

The Moral Foundation
of Political Economy

Joshua P. Hochschild
University of Notre Dame

Beginning in the eighteenth and continuing through the nineteenth century, a great number of volumes were published in Europe and America on the subject of "political economy," which, according to a typical definition, treats "the laws which regulate the production, distribution, and consumption of the material products which have exchangeable value, and which are either necessary, useful, or agreeable to man."[1] But while it is generally thought that political economy is a relatively recent concern, owing both its method and its subject matter to various revolutions in science, politics, and industry, there is an account of political economy far older than the age of Enlightenment. It belongs to the most ancient philosophies and religions, and was applicable even before the rise of manufacture and the development of the modern nation-state. It is captured in the traditional prayer by which Christians recognize that not only spiritual health but even worldly necessities – "our daily bread" – are gifts from God; and while it would thus seem to be more a matter of "faith" than of "science," it is based on its own version of empirical observation and inference:

> Consider the lilies of the field, how they grow; they toil not, neither do they spin; and yet I say unto you, that even Solomon in all his glory was not arrayed like one of these. Wherefore, if God so clothe the grass of the field, which today is, and tomorrow is cast into the oven, shall he not much more clothe you, O ye of little faith? (Matthew 6:28–30)

1

Human beings are creatures of God, according to this account, and must depend upon God for the provision of their material goods. In this religious conviction, we have not just a theology, but an ethic, and the ethic is one which concerns specifically the satisfaction of human wants and needs. It is for this reason that we can say that it is a version of *political economy*, an account which bears on our understanding of the nature and causes of the wealth of nations.

But if the original "invisible hand" – the first-hypothesized hidden cause of the increase and order of human goods – was the providential hand of God, of course the "invisible hand" which is more often remembered is the one associated with Adam Smith's *Inquiry into the Nature and Causes of the Wealth of Nations*: the blind hand of the unregulated market. Against popular mercantilist theories about the management of general economic welfare, Smith discerned in practice, and explained in principle, the unplanned benefits of free trade and exchange, the natural fruitfulness of economic competition. "By pursuing his own interest," Smith famously argued, a man "frequently promotes that of the society more effectually than when he really intends to promote it." While such a man "intends only his own gain," he is nonetheless "led by an invisible hand to promote an end" – the general welfare of the public – "which was no part of his intention."[2]

While the old religions and the old philosophies emphasized the divine mechanism in the ordering of human goods, Smith and the new political economists who followed him turned their attention to human mechanisms. Without denying the reality of these human mechanisms, some religious men, perceiving a tension between human sciences and faith, have accordingly criticized the new science of political economy as another secular threat to spiritual piety. The learned religious and political thinker, Orestes Brownson, for instance, was quick to condemn the theories of Adam Smith, along with socialism, as secular forces competing with Christianity for the attention of men's souls; in the middle of the nineteenth century, Brownson wrote:

> For the last three hundred years, we have lost or been losing our faith in God, in heaven, in love, in justice, in eternity, and been acquiring faith only in human philosophies, in mere theories concerning supply and demand, wealth of nations, self-supporting, labor-saving gov-

ernments; needing no virtue, wisdom, love, sacrifice, or heroism on the part of their managers; working out for us a new Eden, converting all the earth into an Eldorado land, and enabling us all to live in Eden Regained.[3]

Brownson's judgment is severe, and yet it is easy to see how he could regard Smith's "philosophy" as a threat to faith. By claiming that the health and wealth of nations is the natural result of competing individual interests, Smith's theory could be construed as justifying both a radical anthropology, according to which struggle is the most basic human condition, and a dangerous ethic, according to which selfishness becomes the most basic human motive. Smith's defense of market competition could thus be associated with the cruelest social Darwinism, advocating vulgar and brutal greed as the principal virtue. This is why Brownson saw in the new political economy a heretical ethic of material appetite which threatened the true and healthy ethic of humility and sacrifice.

However, even if it is true that Adam Smith's theory has been for many an occasion for the temptation to love money instead of God, this alone does not indicate a necessary conflict between the new emphasis on the human mechanisms at work in the ordering of worldly goods and the old emphasis on the divine. Lord Acton, like Brownson, was a Catholic and anti-socialist, and recognized that man cannot serve both God and Mammon. But unlike Brownson, Acton perceived that one could condemn the worship of Mammon and yet still recognize the validity of Smith's social and economic observations.

Moreover, Lord Acton perceived in Smith's economic observations not the assumption of selfishness and vice, but an affirmation of the central importance of discipline and virtue. Thus, Acton actually found substantial agreement between the new and old political economies, and asserted that, "the doctrine of self-reliance and self-denial, which is the foundation of political economy, [is] written as legibly in the New Testament as in the *Wealth of Nations*."[4]

To understand how Lord Acton could see an ethical "doctrine" as the foundation of modern political economy, it is helpful to remember that the central theme of his lecture on the "History of Freedom in Antiquity" is the relationship of liberty and duty. Acton made it clear that the "doctrine of self-reliance and self-denial" follows on the ethical apprehension of duty – it is the obligation to something other than the self that provides a non-selfish, and non-coercive, motive for action.

A sense of duty can follow from status, rank, or class, but it can also follow from the apprehension of higher principles, and, according to Acton, this apprehension is emancipating. It is ultimately only by appeal to the authority of higher principles that men can secure claims to individual liberty against various worldly forces that threaten it. Acton credited the Stoic philosophers for recognizing this first:

> It is the Stoics who emancipated mankind from its subjugation to despotic rule, and whose enlightened and elevated views bridged the chasm that separates the ancient from the Christian state, and led the way to Freedom. . . . They made it known that there is a will superior to the collective will of man, and a law that overrules those of Solon and Lycurgus. Their test of good government is its conformity to principles that can be traced to a higher legislator. That which we must obey, that to which we are bound to reduce all civil authorities, and to sacrifice every earthly interest, is that immutable law which is perfect and eternal as God Himself, which proceeds from His nature, and reigns over heaven and earth and over all the nations.[5]

Appeal to higher principles, to a higher legislator, both "emancipates" and moves us to "sacrifice earthly interests." According to Acton, "the greater the strength of duty, the greater the strength of liberty." The source of duty, what "creates and strengthens the notion of duty," is religion.

Here it is important to point out how radically Acton differs from those philosophers, like John Stuart Mill, who perceived a fundamental "struggle between Liberty and Authority."[6] Acton viewed liberty and authority not only as compatible but as mutually dependent. While Mill attributes a utilitarian value to religion and authority, realizing that they can be instruments for maintaining order, he ultimately sees them as threats to liberty. Liberty, according to Mill, was the ability to act without impediment, valued because of the sovereignty of the human will, a will thus permitted to exercise itself for any object so long as it does not cause "harm to others."[7]

For Acton, however, "liberty is not the power of doing what we like, but the right of being able to do what we ought." Mill could not agree with Acton that the value of liberty is inseparable from standards of moral duty, in part because Mill founded his own ethical theory on the "Greatest Happiness principle," by which human actions are understood as aimed not at what is good, but at what is pleasurable. Mill thus committed the fundamental error of confusing the psychological and metaphysical orders; rather than asserting that something should be desired because it is good, Mill maintained that something is justifiably regarded as good because it is desired. This leaves Mill without any standard of evaluation besides the subjective, and capricious, human appetite.

Acton, on the other hand, knew that moral convictions cannot be reduced to feeling or appetite. When he spoke of "duty," he did not, like Mill, believe that duty was simply "a feeling in our own mind, a pain, more or less intense."[8] For Acton, duty was not moral *feeling*, but moral *obligation*; it involved genuine ethical commitment, and was measured by a real standard of evaluation independent of human taste and appetite. Thus, in an even clearer association of the New Testament and the *Wealth of Nations*, Acton wrote:

> The moral foundation of political economy is not the satisfaction of appetite but the fulfillment of duties. Labour, patience, justice, peace, and self-denial are the mainsprings of economical production, and the metaphysical basis of the science is not in a philosophy which reduces religion and science to mere satisfaction of an appetite, like eating or drinking, but in the verification of the promise, "Seek ye first the kingdom of God and His justice and all these things" – the necessaries of life – "shall be added unto you."

As Lord Acton understands, the new principles of political economy amounted to a practical confirmation of the religious conviction that prosperity was the reward of virtues – such as humility, patience, and self-denial – which are fostered by dedication to permanent, transcendent ideals. The principles of *laissez-faire* economics do not promote a selfish social Darwinism, but affirm the values of discipline and sacrifice; these are the virtues of "self-reliance and self-denial" proper to free and responsible individuals, virtues which follow from religious commitment to an end beyond this world – "the kingdom of God" – and which make possible the ordered, peaceful, and prosperous maintenance of a free society.

Notes

1. John McVickar, *Outlines of Political Economy* (New York: Wilder and Campbell, 1825), 7.

2. Adam Smith, *An Inquiry into the Nature and Causes of the Wealth of Nations* (London: Oxford University Press, 1976), vol. 1, 456 (bk. IV, ch. 2, ¶ 9).

3. Orestes Brownson, "The Present State of Society," *Democratic Review* 13, no. 61 (July, 1843), 25; reprinted in *Orestes Brownson: Selected Political Essays*, ed. Russell Kirk (New Brunswick: Transaction Publishers, 1990), 35–36.

4. "The History of Freedom in Antiquity," in *Selected Writings of Lord Acton*, J. Rufus Fears, ed., vol. 1, *Essays in the History of Liberty* (Indianapolis: Liberty Classics, 1985), 27.

5. Ibid., 23–24.

6. John Stuart Mill, *On Liberty*, in *On Liberty, Representative Government, The Subjection of Women: Three Essays by John Stuart Mill* (London: Oxford University Press, 1912), 5.

7. Ibid., 14–15: "The object of this essay is to assert one very simple principle, as entitled to govern absolutely the dealings of society with the individual in the way of compulsion and control, whether the means used by physical force in the form of legal penalties, or the moral coercion of public opinion. That principle is, that the sole end for which mankind are warranted, individually or collectively, in interfering with the liberty of action of any of their number, is self-protection. That the only purpose for which power can be rightfully exercised over any member of a civilized community, against his will, is to prevent harm to others. His own good, either physical or moral, is not a sufficient warrant. He cannot rightfully be compelled to do or forbear because it will be better for him to do so, because it will make him happier, because, in the opinions of others, to do so would be wise, or even right. . . . Over himself, over his own body and mind, the individual is sovereign."

8. John Stuart Mill, *Utilitarianism*, in *Mill's Ethical Writings*, J. B. Schneewind, ed. (New York: Collier Books, 1965), 302.

The Kingdom of Man in America: Economic Freedom and Prosperity in Moral and Theological Perspective

Zachary R. Calo

University of Pennsylvania

A God without wrath brought men without sin into a kingdom without judgment through the ministrations of a Christ without a cross.
—H. Richard Niebuhr[1]

When H. Richard Niebuhr composed these words, he was responding to the theology of liberal Christians who denied the innate sinfulness of humankind. The position of liberal theologians was that corrupt social institutions were the cause of sin, and the imperfections of humankind were to be overcome not through the work and forgiveness of God, but through the actions of properly trained elites who could direct the transformation of society. Advocates of this position generally abandoned notions of God as the omnipotent Lord who opened the doors of His kingdom through the life and resurrection of Jesus Christ. After all, had not humanity progressed to a point where it could move beyond belief in God's redemption and instead focus on humanity redeeming itself? There was no need for a kingdom of God when there was the possibility of creating a kingdom of Man.

It is a tragedy that the church needed neo-orthodox theologians like the Niebuhrs, Barth, Tillich, Brunner, and Bonhoeffer to bring attention to the most fundamental teachings of sin and redemption. In a century that Michael Novak calls "history's bloodiest," an era in which "the bodies of individuals have been thrown around like sacks of bones," one might anticipate that the legacy of Hitler, Stalin, Mussolini, and Mao would provoke humanity into remembering the

7

potential it possesses for grave evil.[2] Yet, understanding sin requires a commitment to truth and judgment, and during a century in which truth has become relativity and freedom an invitation to unfettered autonomy, little room remains for the inconvenient concept of sin. Flattered with its own success in generating new wealth and knowledge, humanity has seen little need for God, especially a God whose truth might challenge the ways of this world. People of the twentieth century have forsaken the legacy and traditions of the past with brazen confidence. And while this desire to look beyond the present to envision a new and different reality has indeed produced many important developments, by abandoning the God of truth and the truth of God, modern society has destroyed the very foundation upon which its prosperity rests.

Lord Acton's writings frequently emphasize that liberty cannot be based on the satisfaction of individual appetite. The benefits and privileges that freedom creates are wholly dependent on meeting the obligations and sacrifices that freedom requires. This perspective is captured in Acton's statement that "liberty is not the power of doing what we like, but the right of being able to do what we ought."[3] Alan Keyes recently articulated a similar position when he stated that "freedom is not another kind of empty licentiousness." Freedom, in other words, does not grant people "the right to do what is wrong."[4] Nevertheless, while a few public voices still discuss the moral foundations of freedom to which Acton was so committed, Western society has largely abandoned the idea that a self-governing people need special virtues. Truth and virtue are concepts that the media ignores and academic culture despises. Sadly, even many leaders within the church, an institution traditionally consulted for moral guidance, now fail to speak of ethical commitment with any certainty or conviction.[5]

In the end, liberty cannot exist apart from truth, and truth cannot exist apart from God. Christian thinkers throughout history have affirmed the importance of recognizing that knowledge cannot come merely from philosophical inquiry, but must rest in an understanding of the true God. Lesslie Newbigin writes, for example, that Augustine's famous slogan, *credo ut intelligam*, "I believe in order that I may know," characterizes faith "as the pathway to knowledge."[6] It is certainly not the case that all people in a nation-state must profess allegiance to God in order for freedom to prosper.[7] Yet, at the same time, freedom must be based on truth and obligation or else it will tumble into moral anarchy and political tyranny. The danger of modern times is that many leaders and intellectuals have rejected what the Declaration of Independence identifies as the foundation of liberty: "The Laws of nature and nature's God." Though Thomas Jefferson, the author of this phrase, was a deist who rejected orthodox understandings of biblical morality, he nevertheless understood that freedom could not exist apart from the foundation of "laws" and truth.[8] Michael Novak makes this point when he writes simply that "*Truth Matters.*"[9] However, in the age of postmodern relativism and philosophical deconstructionism, where the very existence of objective truth is denied, humanity has become the ultimate arbiter of what is right and good.[10] When humanity, rather than God, assumes this responsibility, "the fulfillment of duties" that Acton views as the moral foundation of political economy dissolves into little more than individual pragmatism and the "satisfaction of appetite."[11]

The very concept of political economy attests to the interrelationship of political and economic processes. As Friedrich Hayek and Milton Friedman have argued, economic freedom cannot exist without supportive political institutions; similarly, economic freedom is an essential component in preserving political freedom. Nevertheless, while many people acknowledge the link between economics and government, few speak of the moral foundation they have in common. In recent times, significant attention has indeed been given to the overall moral crisis in American culture. However, this crisis is often portrayed as a problem that is not relevant to economic concerns. The way in which people are separately characterized as cultural conservatives and economic conservatives clearly illustrates the failure of society to recognize that economics is a moral discipline. Economic production cannot simply be dismissed as a purely utilitarian practice that has no inherent moral qualities. As Acton so clearly and rightfully argues, political economy, like freedom itself, cannot prosper apart from a strong moral basis.

Economic production is not an amoral activity, but is in its essence a just and proper undertaking that honors the freedom and creativity granted humanity by the Creator. As the twentieth century has demonstrated, a free society and a free economy can produce magnificent results. However, while the benefits of these advances have been undeniable, the "mainsprings of economical production" – the virtues of labor, patience, justice, peace, and self-denial – have been largely destroyed by humanity's greed and inflated sense of self-worth. The true moral foundation of political economy has been weakened by what Michael Novak refers to as the "many allurements" of prosperity.[12] In the midst of great wealth, knowledge, and achievement, humanity has forgotten its own creatureliness. The same confidence in humanity that inspired liberal theology's vision of an earthly kingdom has infiltrated the whole of society. The love of God is displayed powerfully in the opportunity humanity has to utilize the resources of creation in economic productivity. Yet, while humanity may assume the role of co-creator, it is still subject to the truth and will of the one Creator.

Economic prosperity has not only had the negative effect of encouraging the satisfaction of individual appetite, but it has also obfuscated the duty of charity and the relationship of the poor to political economy. Complex and extensive welfare states now exist in virtually every industrialized nation, and while many of these efforts are well intentioned, the current philosophical justification for government involvement in providing for the poor ultimately works to destroy freedom and prosperity. I am not contending that there is no place for cooperative efforts to assist the poor or that the government must in no way involve itself in social welfare activities.[13] Rather, I am bringing attention to the dangerous notion that individuals have a *right* to public assistance. Robert Sirico writes that work can be seen "from a theological perspective, as a moral duty for those who can do it."[14] Denying people the right to work and earn commensurate reward is as great a moral blight on society as allowing the poor to suffer in the face of affluence. The assumption that all people must share equally in the results of economic prosperity ignores the fact that, as free creatures, people will receive different rewards based, at least in part, on the different choices they make. Society should not return to the days of poor laws and poorhouses when impoverished individuals were immediately branded as morally inferior and in need of uplifting by the better classes. Nor, however, should society support a welfare system that discourages people from experiencing the importance of patience and labor. True self-worth comes not from a guaranteed handout, but only when one is afforded the opportunity to become a productive contributor in the shaping of creation.

The growth of the welfare state has also contributed to the destruction of charitable compassion. Studies continue to show that Americans give generously. Yet, when assisting the poor is viewed as a problem for the government, people are discouraged from experiencing the true importance of self-denial and the sharing of creation's bounty. A free nation cannot survive when individuals choose to put the self first, without regard to needs of community and society. American society has become rather schizophrenic about how it views the poor. On one hand, people believe that society has a moral responsibility, through government, to help the impoverished. On the other, individuals all too often act as if the reality of poverty need not change their sense of personal obligation. In a time of great affluence, when feelings of sufficiency apart from God emerge all too easily, people more than ever need to realize that economics is not "like eating or drinking," but is a deeply moral and spiritual activity. Producing and giving are activities that allow individuals to participate with God in the work of creation.

In the end, the only remedy for many of these societal problems is a new commitment to truth. Political and economic freedom cannot exist without a moral foundation, and the understanding of this moral foundation comes only from knowledge of God. Equally important, however, is that in an age of new and rapidly developing knowledge, society must recognize that certain things cannot be known. Humanity will never completely master this world. No discovery, social program, or economic miracle will be able to free this world and its people from the wages of sin and death. The kingdom of Man will never be, for the fullness of prosperity will come only with the reign of God's eternal kingdom.

Notes

1. H. Richard Niebuhr, *The Kingdom of God in America* (New York: Harper and Row, 1959), 193.

2. Michael Novak, "Awakening from Nihilism: The Templeton Prize Address," in *First Things* 45 (August/September 1994).

3. Michael Novak demonstrates how the modern liberal project has rejected Acton's vision. Novak writes that "In recent decades especially, at least in the United States, 'liberal' has come to be associated both with a radical individualism and with an insistence on doing not what one ought to do, but what one feels like doing." Quotation from *The Catholic Ethic and the Spirit of Capitalism* (New York: Free Press, 1993), 197.

4. This quotation comes from a speech Keyes delivered in New Hampshire on February 19, 1995, as part of his presidential campaign. Though the speech is unpublished, it was broadcast February 22, 1995, on the radio program *Focus on the Family*.

5. Thomas Reeve's study *The Empty Church: The Suicide of Liberal Christianity* (New York: Free Press, 1996) demonstrates persuasively the link between liberal theology and the declining moral authority of mainstream churches in American society. In a time when technology and pluralism are presenting new and complex moral questions, many churches cannot agree on basic fundamental ethical principles, much less be in a position to offer moral leadership.

6. Lesslie Newbigin, *Truth and Authority in Modernity* (Valley Forge, Pa.: Trinity Press International, 1996), 3.

7. A major debate in the church today is over the role specifically Christian ethics can play in society. Some theologians, such as Stanley Hauerwas, contend that the basis of Christian ethics is so unique that true virtue and ethics cannot exist outside of the church. I believe this perspective falls short because it does not recognize the role foundational ethics must play in the sustentation of a free society. While freedom need not be based solely on Christian morality, basic human rights will not continue to exist "without enduring theological foundations such as the doctrines of *imago dei*, the grace of reason, the providential orders of society . . . Modern, secular theorists kept the flower but threw out the root ideas, a development that made human rights appear more groundless than they were." The Judeo-Christian tradition must continue to assert its moral force if freedom is to survive. The above quotation comes from Max L. Stackhouse, "In the Company of Hauerwas," *Journal for Christian Theological Research* 2:1 (1997).

8. Marvin Olasky's study *Fighting for Liberty and Virtue: Political and Cultural Wars in Eighteenth-Century America* (Washington: Regnery, 1996) is an illuminating study of the role that religion and values played in the political debates of colonial and early republic America. This perspective is largely absent in

other historical scholarship in this field. See especially chapter 6, "Virtue, Vice, and the Battlefield."

9. Novak, "Awakening from Nihilism." Italics in original.

10. An especially helpful article is J. Bottum, "Christians and Postmoderns," in *First Things* 40 (February 1994), 28–32. Bottum presents a revealing analysis of the relationship between medieval Christian philosophers and contemporary postmodernists. "The premoderns said that without God, there would be no knowledge, and the postmoderns say we have no God and have no knowledge." See also, Carl F. H. Henry, "Natural Law and Nihilistic Culture" in *First Things* 49 (January 1995), 55–60.

11. Phillip E. Johnson's study, *Reason in the Balance: The Case Against Naturalism in Science, Law, and Education* (Downers Grove, Ill.: InterVarsity Press, 1995) describes the dangerous moral consequences that have resulted from the influence of naturalism and nihilism. Both Johnson and Michael Novak, in *The Catholic Ethic and the Spirit of Capitalism*, discuss Richard Rorty's neo-pragmatic philosophy. Rorty denies that holding no foundation in God or reason leads to moral anarchy, yet as Novak writes, it is much easier to hold these views when one "has not been put to the test" (198) of responding to totalitarianism.

12. Novak, *The Catholic Ethic and the Spirit of Capitalism*, 196.

13. See, for example, Peter L. Berger and Richard John Neuhaus, *To Empower People: The Role of Mediating Structures in Public Policy* (Washington: American Enterprise Institute for Public Policy Research, 1977). Berger and Neuhaus contend that the welfare state is so well established that the direction of public policy should not be to advocate dismantling the entire infrastructure, but rather transfer resources through more humane and effective community organizations.

14. Robert A. Sirico, "Work is Moral and So Is Workfare," *New York Times*, 27 July 1997.

The Moral Foundation of Civilization: Appetite or Duty?

Jonathan Barlow
Covenant Theological Seminary

> The moral foundation of political economy is not the satisfaction of appetite but the fulfillment of duties. Labour, patience, justice, peace, and self-denial are the mainsprings of economical production, and the metaphysical basis of the science is not in a philosophy which reduces religion and science to mere satisfaction of an appetite, like eating or drinking, but in the verification of the promise, "Seek ye first the kingdom of God and His justice and all these things" – the necessaries of life – "shall be added unto you."
>
> –Lord Acton

Seek first his kingdom and His righteousness . . ." Do these startling and counter-intuitive words of Christ[1] urge His disciples to attend to the transcendent as an aid to accomplishing the mundane? No, they instruct humans to view every mundane activity from the perspective of the transcendent. The former interpretation makes even religion the "satisfaction of an appetite." The latter makes religion the metaphysical basis for all aspects of life, especially those civilizations which humans create. The kingdom is both the end that all activities should seek and the organizing reality – the worldview – in terms of which all activities should be conducted.

Acton linked the pursuance of the kingdom to the concept of duty, as set over against appetite. The great question for our age is whether or not a civilization can succeed if the only duty it accepts is the obligation created by its own appetite. Acton's concept of duty is clearly oriented toward the obligation that humans have to a transcendent reality – God's law. In this essay, we will examine the nature and fruit of the modern tendency toward naturalism and its companion ethic, appetite. Then, we will contrast this view with the supernaturalism evidenced in Acton's quote and its companion ethic, duty. Our discussion will argue that only a civilization which is founded upon the principle that humans are obligated to a personal, extramundane God can be free to seek mundane prosperity.

No one in recent years has more clearly isolated and critiqued the hegemony of naturalism in the academy, in science, and in law than Berkeley law professor Phillip E. Johnson. In his first book on this subject, *Darwin on Trial*,[2] Johnson argues against the theory of evolution on a number of bases. His chief criticism of the theory, however, is that Darwinism, far from being the epitome of "science," is actually the last refuge naturalistic philosophy has found for explaining just about everything that was previously explained with reference to transcendent realities. Of course, such critiques are not new. C. S. Lewis criticized materialism[3] as "nothing buttery"[4]: the human mind is "nothing but" the brain; love is "nothing but" an epiphenomenon of chemical reactions in the brain, etc.[5] As the quote from Lord Acton above illustrates, he, too, would have railed against those who see civil ethics as "nothing but" the satisfaction of appetites. In his second book, *Reason in the Balance*,[6] Johnson goes beyond the theory of evolution and critiques naturalism itself, showing successfully that academic "nothing-buttery" has excluded any transcendent explanations from credibility. His goal is to demonstrate that there can be a distinction between science (reason) and naturalism. To equate the two is, in fact, an irrational and arbitrary bias or pre-commitment, rather than the result of reasoned inquiry.

Johnson's critique, and the ensuing movement which has produced such figures as Michael Behe and Stephen Meyer, is encouraging. It represents a reaction to "nothing-buttery" that may someday serve to topple this sleeping giant from its dogmatic dominance. The reason this is germane to Lord Acton's comments above on the moral foundations of political economy is that Acton contrasts "the satisfaction of an appetite" with the concept of duty. Naturalistic accounts of human ethics almost invariably reduce to the satisfaction of an appetite. Only supernatural accounts of moral obligation, in which persons have an obligation to God and to the image of God borne by fellow men, can escape appetite as the basis for civilization.

This fact is illustrated well by Richard Dawkins, one target of Phillip Johnson's critique, who is probably the most strident proponent of evolutionary and naturalistic theory today. His self-conscious reduction of everything to its constituent, physical elements leads him to deny the most intuitive of ethical principles. When asked what moral justification could be given for condemning some "lads" who "break into an old man's house and kill him," Dawkins says he could only offer the following response: "This is not a society in which I wish to live. Without having a rational reason for it necessarily, I'm going to do whatever I can to stop you doing this." The interviewer counters wryly, "They'll say, 'This is the society we want to live in.'" Dawkins responds, "I couldn't, ultimately, argue intellectually against somebody who did something I found obnoxious. I think I could finally only say, 'Well, in this society you can't get away with it' and call the police."[7] While most materialists are thankfully not as consistent as Dawkins, Dawkins's epistemological self-consciousness serves to get the naturalist position onto the table – and what we see is certainly ugly. A civilization founded upon "nothing but" the appetites and preferences of individual citizens is a feral and destructive one. Dawkins fails to confront adequately that even his distaste for the killing of an old man stems from the Judeo-Christian moral foundation that he has imbibed almost automatically from his youth in Britain. Yes, perhaps Dawkins's culturally sanctified appetites could sustain a civilization for a time, but as the rug of transcendent restraint is slowly pulled out from under it, the results would look more like Stalinist Russia than the humanist utopia of Walden Two.

Why is naturalism necessarily the companion of non-theistic accounts of ethics? The words of Jesus, quoted by Acton, provide us with the answer. Jesus' famous admonition to "seek the kingdom first" comes as the summary of a section of the Sermon on the Mount in which he tells the disciples not to worry – not to worry about what one will eat or drink or wear tomorrow. Of course Jesus was not teaching that one should become an ascetic or a "ne'er do well." On the contrary, he was simply speaking against those who show their distrust of

God by constantly fretting about material things. Jesus then drew a distinction between those who seek first material things (appetites) and those who seek first the things of God. He goes further and says that the latter will then have those material things added to them as well. Jesus provides His perspective upon what is truly important. The material needs and appetites of life are not all there is, nor even all that there primarily is. What seems so important to humans for the furthering of civilization is but a natural (supernatural?) result of seeking the end of furthering the Kingdom of God. For the naturalist, however, the appetites are "all that is," and even love for fellow man is "nothing-buttery."

It is impossible, it seems, to associate duty with anything but obligation to persons – even duty to country, when that concept is isolated, emerges as duty to the people who make up a country.[8] Naturalistic philosophy removes the intrinsic significance of human persons by making them merely very successful animals, and it completely removes the transcendent significance of the absolute person, God. If duty is always personal in nature, and there is no absolute person, then there can be no absolute duty. The antithesis is clear, and it is because of God's preserving grace that naturalists are inconsistent with their philosophy; yes, even Dawkins.

The alternative to naturalism is supernaturalism, the perspective presupposed in Acton's quote. We have seen that in the absence of a religious worldview, ethical obligation reduces to what Acton described as a "mere satisfaction of an appetite." A religious worldview, however, described in terms of the character of an absolute person, God, creates covenantal obligation of an absolute character. In order to take up Acton's challenge of verifying the promise of Jesus, we have but one hurdle to jump: the various criticisms offered against theistic ethics.

The major criticism leveled at religious accounts of morality briefly follows: if what is good is what God wills, then the possibility of God changing His will compromises the absolute character of moral good. Another objection finds an early expression in Plato's *Euthypro*, a dialogue in which Socrates asks whether what God commands is right because God commands it, or whether God commands it because it is right. Is God's will in subjection to an impersonal definition of good? Surely we have seen that such impersonal standards are simply not available.[9] Then, the only objection which remains is that God's will is arbitrary. If God should decide to rescind the sixth commandment, then murder becomes morally good, or at least morally neutral. Though Acton himself was a student of Plato, it is here where Acton's worldview differs (and emerges as stronger) because of his Christian theism. Plato attempted to solve this problem of the *Euthypro* by positing impersonal "forms" that transcend even the gods, and that fall into the problem all impersonal accounts of ethics face. Christianity, however, posits God's character – His attributes, which never change, and which hold His will captive. It is certainly not any limitation upon God to say that His will is in perfect conformity with His character. Thus, we may answer Socrates by saying that what God commands is right because his commands always conform to his character. In addition, God is able to reveal His character and commands to humanity. Plato's forms are mute idols, covenantally irrelevant, and epistemologically unavailable.[10]

Now that we have seen that the only real source of justification for the concept of duty arises from a religious perspective, it is a small step to suggest that only a civilization founded upon such transcendent (yet personal) standards can provide a rational defense of its principles. Humans then cease to be the most successful animals so far in evolutionary history, and emerge as beings specially created in the image of God, in a covenantal relationship with covenantal obligations. Duty to God and duty to fellow humans, the essence of the "two tables" of the decalogue, provide the foundation for a civil society. In seeking first the kingdom of God and His righteousness, we escape both prideful, Nietzschean individualism and soul-killing collectivism. By providing a source of ethical verification which transcends the state itself, religious ethics destroy any kind of "might makes right" claim on the part of magistrates.

We have observed that Lord Acton was really making a distinction between two completely different world and life views. One, which we observed to rest upon the presupposition of naturalism, reduces ethical obligation to the mere satisfaction of an appetite and provides no foundation for a successful and free civilization. The other, however, which rests upon the presupposition of supernaturalism, provides a covenantal basis for ethical obligation between humans and their Creator. This religious perspective not only provides an intellectually defensible set of criteria for moral action, but it guards against individualism and collectivism – the most significant failure of naturalistic accounts of ethics.

Does this commit us and Lord Acton to theocracy? Only philosophically. Any form of government which justifies its structure and role by reference to transcendent ethical systems is in a sense "theocratic," because God's moral will is instrumental in policy decisions. However, when we Westerners imagine a theocracy, we are often actually picturing an ecclesiocracy in which the church rules both itself and the civil government. This is far from what the framers of the American form of government, for instance, had in mind. Separation of church government from civil government is necessary to avoid the hegemony of any one sect or denomination. Separation of religious ethics from civil government, however, is simply impossible, since no other ethical standards are available. Thus, a form of "principled pluralism" seems to be the form of government most commended to us. The government is not free from religion, then, for such "freedom" is always simply slavery to the appetites of the masses. It is, however, free from religious despots who would destroy the freedom that God has granted all people, even irreligious people, under His law.

Thus, far from limiting liberty, religion provides the only conceptual framework in terms of which liberty can be justified, and civilizations can succeed.

Notes

1. Matthew 6:33.

2. Phillip E. Johnson, *Darwin on Trial* (Downers Grove, Ill.: InterVarsity Press, 1991).

3. Philosophically, materialism (or "physicalism") is the belief that everything which exists is physical. This metaphysical sense of the word is to be distinguished from the slightly different use of the term by political (Marxian) or value theorists. The metaphysical use of materialism does, however, affect these areas, as we shall see.

4. Cited in George Gilder, "The Materialist Superstition," *The Intercollegiate Review* 31, no. 2 (Spring 1996).

5. See also the symposium sponsored by the Intercollegiate Studies Institute on "The Death of Materialism and the Renewal of Culture" which appeared in *The Intercollegiate Review* 31, no. 2 (Spring 1996).

6. Phillip E. Johnson, *Reason in the Balance* (Downers Grove, Ill.: InterVarsity Press, 1995).

7. Nick Pollard, "The Simple Answer (Interview with Richard Dawkins)," *Third Way* (April 1995): 15–19.

8. This notion, that ethical obligation is always personal, cannot be argued at length here. The reader is referred to the fine discussion of this point by John Frame, *Apologetics to the Glory of God* (Phillipsburg, N.J.: P & R Publishing, 1994), 97–102. Briefly, the authority of absolute moral principles can either come from personal or impersonal sources. If we answer that it comes from impersonal sources, we are positing an "impersonal structure or law in the universe" (98). But, if the laws of the universe are at base chance, as the naturalist holds them to be, then what kind of ethical obligation can be learned "from the random collisions of subatomic particles? What loyalty do we owe to pure chance?" (ibid.). Frame argues that since impersonal sources of ethical obligation all fail to provide us with a credible explanation for ethical obligation, we must turn to the realm of the personal. He writes, "Obligations and loyalties arise in the context of interpersonal relationships . . . obligations, loyalties, and therefore morality are covenantal in character" (98–99). God, then, as the absolute person, also provides a solution to the subjectivity of lesser personal obligations. Thus, one can choose, for instance, between loyalty to the people of his or her country and the people of his or her family based upon the absolute loyalty one has to God.

9. See endnote 8.

10. For a rigorous defense of so-called "Divine Command Ethics" the reader is referred to Richard Mouw, *The God Who Commands*, (Notre Dame: Notre Dame Press, 1990).

Deep Moral Foundations:
The Keys to Stable and Prosperous
Political Economies

Michael Black
Mount Saint Mary's Seminary

The quotation upon which this paper is based is a tightly packed, concise statement, the content of which could be richly mined in various directions. The relationship and interaction that exists between the political economy and the moral life is at the quotation's core, however, and is the concept which this paper hopes to explore.

In the quote, there is a presupposition that a political economy has a foundation, something which is not self-evident to those who unthinkingly divide society into only political and economic spheres. The very idea that the political-economic order relies on any foundation whatsoever is a concept as overlooked as it is important. The presumption that political systems and economic orders are self-creating, and that they themselves protect the common good and regulate commercial exchange, is an erroneous ideal. In reality, these two spheres of human activity depend upon a multitude of factors outside of their control to even come into existence. One could say that political economies owe their existence and subsequent form to the particular conditions which precede their establishment, conditions fundamental to the creation of the "preexisting social bonds that make governments and markets possible."[1]

The whole range of fundamental preconditions needed to form a society healthy enough to support a political economy create the foundation of that society, not those institutions which are better said to be its effluence. As with all other foundations, this one, too, must be constructed previous to that of the structures which rest upon it, making it both a separate entity and yet something absolutely vital to all that comes after it. Because it inherently serves as an independent and a supporting structure at the same time, an eroding foundation can cause any structure resting upon it, regardless of that structure's own particular integrity, to collapse. Highly developed, complex economies and governments with long histories of success need not, then, continue on their paths of stability solely because of well-established records of accomplishment. If the factors which precipitated their formation and growth lie outside the control of the governmental and economic institutions themselves, then those same factors could lead to the end of those same institutions despite the latter's relative health. The foundation of a society is of the highest importance, then, in that the survival of innumerable other goods, including political and economic ones, are linked to its soundness.

The quotation is correct in recognizing that this all-important societal foundation is a moral one, and a moral foundation concerned with the fulfillment of duties rather than the mere satisfaction of appetites. To state that the satisfaction of appetite is not an adequate moral foundation borders, in fact, on being tautologous. The satisfaction of an appetite like eating or drinking cannot stand opposite the fulfillment of duty as an opposing option in any moral decision because acts such as eating and drinking cannot be said, under normal conditions, to even be moral acts. A moral action can be called good precisely because it could have been called bad; that is, the possibility of choosing the good or the bad is part of what makes certain decisions moral ones. The choice to eat, drink, sleep, etc., is not a choice with options in the moral sense. To satisfy these appetites is actually a prerequisite to even being a moral agent, as only living human beings are such, and the negation of these appetites would cause the cessation of the moral agent, i.e. death.

Having posited that a moral foundation is fundamental to the establishment of a political economy, a look at what that foundation consists of is now in order. As stated in the quotation, the fulfillment of duties is at the heart of society's moral foundation, especially considering that the satisfaction of appetite normally does not even fall under the category of a moral action. The fulfillment of a duty is not in and of itself a virtue; rather, its end must be considered to determine its moral quality. It is not hard to imagine examples where a person would feel the duty to carry out an immoral act because of fear, a promise, a misguided conscience, a reward, etc. Contrariwise, the type of duty that fosters the acquisition of virtue is the duty directed towards a good end, whether it be God, self, or neighbor. Duty, then, can be a seedbed for virtue when the ends worked for are good ones.

The virtues cited in the quotation – labor, patience, justice, peace, and self-denial – along with others, are indeed good when done for good ends and can also be mainsprings of economical production. They not only bring order and peace into one's interior life, but also produce tangible benefits in the economic realm. The person who works patiently and diligently while denying himself some of life's small pleasures will produce more at a higher quality or serve more customers in a conscientious manner than the person who does not cultivate these or similar virtues. It would seem to go without saying that he who seeks to better himself rather than "find" himself will succeed in dominating the job he holds to such an extent that it cannot but reward his efforts very richly.

While virtue does produce goods in the economic realm, these goods are better understood to be a part of those things which "shall be added unto you" after first seeking the kingdom of God. It is in the fulfillment of religious duty that virtue truly finds its richest meaning. Pope John Paul II has written beautifully on the meaning of human work as a duty for every person, and sees in the myriad virtues found in hard work the true exaltation of the Christian vocation. He says that "man, created in the image of God, shares by his work in the image of the Creator and . . . in a sense continues to develop that activity, and perfects it as he advances further and further in the discovery of the resources and values contained in the whole of creation."[2] He also writes that people "by their labor . . . are unfolding the Creator's work . . . and contributing by their personal industry to the realization in history of the divine plan."[3] Seen thus, work acquires metaphysical significance. It is something much larger than a means of economic exchange. God Himself worked in creating the world, and people, by working, emulate that divine work and even continue it through their domination of nature. As people's manipulation of nature becomes more and more complex, they manifest to a greater and greater degree their dominion over it. Although this dominion can become more technological and removed from the actual resources of the earth itself, it nonetheless never moves outside of the mandate of Genesis to "subdue the earth." In fact, the more advanced this work, or dominion, becomes, the more man shows himself to be a son of God who, through his creation *ex nihilo*, dominates nature in an absolute way. There is no other way for people to subdue the earth apart from work, and by manipulating nature to their advantage, and utilizing the things of the earth for their own ends, people show their superiority to nature. To strive to be perfect as one's Creator is perfect is indeed seeking "first the kingdom of God." The things which "shall be added unto you" are the secondary, but no less real, economic advantages that proceed from this primary human duty to act in the image and likeness of God.

> Creation left to itself is incomplete, and humans are called to be co-creators with God, bringing forth the potentialities the Creator has hidden. Creation is full of secrets waiting to be discovered, riddles which human intelligence is expected by the Creator to unlock. The world did not spring from the hand of God as wealthy as humans might make it.[4]

God expects us to delve into the secrets of nature; He expects us to cultivate great virtue and skill in discovering and unleashing the potentialities hidden in all of creation. The potentialities realized will then spur economic production, for if nature can be "harvested" even when people do not apply themselves to it with skill and virtue, all the greater will be the "harvest" when they do so:

> Locke observed that a field of, say, strawberries, highly favored by nature, left to itself, might produce what seemed to be an abundance of strawberries. Subject to cultivation and care by practical intelligence, however, such a field might be made to produce not simply twice but tenfold as many strawberries.[5]

Such is the relationship between virtue, subduing the earth, and economical production, and it is as applicable to technological societies as it is to agricultural ones.

To seek the kingdom of God is synonymous with seeking virtue. What a person does on earth has value precisely because it is a person who does it, not so much for what is produced. So while certain virtues lead to the accumulation of wealth, knowledge, and other human goods, these things are to be prized only secondarily. Of first import is the fact that these virtues are evidence of progress on the road to God. Even if they were not to produce tangible goods because of a faulty economy or a bad government, these virtues would not lose their essential value. What a person does matters because only a person is a source of virtue, and he is such because only he is truly free and only he is a genuine source of responsibility.

An unvirtuous society would not enjoy economic success despite the greatest of economic principles. Laziness, mendacity, disorder, self-indulgence, and like vices are both antithetical to the seeking of the kingdom of God and the basis for economic disaster. It would perhaps be more accurate to say that these vices are the basis for economic disaster precisely because they are antithetical to the seeking of the kingdom of God. This situation seems to point to the certitude that if a person seeks first the kingdom of the self through self-gratification, self-indulgence, self-interest, etc. the necessaries of life will not only not be added unto him, but they may actually be subtracted. There is no merit in vice or the mere satisfaction of human appetites, neither in heaven nor on earth. Only living a religious life, especially in its moral precepts, will instill the virtues needed to produce economic gain as the superabundance of supernatural virtue.

There may be many who cultivate certain virtues solely for the economic benefits they produce, with no heed to their theological significance, but this in no way eradicates the virtues' theological connections or origins. Regarding only the economic gain associated with a virtue does not deny its religious origin, but only puts a limit on the value that the virtue has been allowed to have by he who has it. The virtue is not diminished, although he who is not aware of its other dimensions may be.

At a more macro level, political economies need people to guide them, and virtuous people are more likely to handle them well than those seeking merely to fulfill an appetite. Political economies should be at mankind's service. They themselves are blind and when put in the wrong hands can be vehicles for great harm. Utopian social projects, unmitigated greed, corruption, exploitation, and worse have led political economies to inflict great pain on those who were supposed to benefit from them. The things of the world are meant to be a tool to advance mankind, and if the "self" in self-government is unvirtuous there is no reason to expect that the government linked to it will be any different.

To conclude, having looked at how seeking to emulate the virtues of God, especially work, can lead to economic productivity, perhaps the final word should be on where a person learns to emulate God, as people are not "noble savages" hard-wired to do the good. We learn virtue, and the school where we learn is the family. The family is a microcosm of society, it is

> a continuous locus of reciprocal obligations that constitute an unending school for moral instruction . . . We learn to cope with the people of this world because we learn to cope with the members of our family. Those who flee the family flee the world; bereft of the former's affection, tutelage, and challenges, they are unprepared for the latter's tests, judgments, and demands.[6]

The problem today is not so much children fleeing parents as parents fleeing children and responsibility. With the decline of the family comes the decline of virtue, the moral foundation essential to any political economy. If we want economic production we also want to do everything in our power to build up families, which are like millions of bricks in the superstructures which support political economies.

Notes

1. James Q. Wilson, *The Moral Sense* (New York: The Free Press, 1995), 15.

2. John Paul II, *Laborem Exercens* (Boston: St. Paul Books & Media), 25.

3. Ibid., 25.

4. Michael Novak, *The Spirit of Democratic Capitalism* (Lanham, Md.: Madison Books, 1991), 39.

5. Ibid., 39.

6. Wilson, *The Moral Sense*, 163.

The Moral Personality of Economics

Sean Mattie
University of Dallas

L ord Acton teaches us that in the discussion of economics, we must not overlook its moral consequences. He writes:

> The moral foundation of political economy is not the satisfaction of appetite but the fulfillment of duties. Labour, patience, justice, peace, and self-denial are the mainsprings of economical production, and the metaphysical basis of the science is not in a philosophy which reduces religion and science to mere satisfaction of an appetite, like eating or drinking, but in the verification of the promise, "Seek ye first the kingdom of God and His justice and all these things" – the necessaries of life – "shall be added unto you."

The emphasis on duties, virtues, and spiritual calling in a statement on political economy testifies that economics ultimately concerns *human* actions. Economic activity is not an impersonal process, but the coordinated efforts of free persons with moral obligations and a transcendent vocation to God. A study of economics that fails to comprehend morality neglects an essential aspect of the person, the true subject of all economic action. Thus, moral anthropology is not extrinsic to economics, but a necessary, integral part of the science. Acton's humane contribution to political economy attests that economics is not ethically neutral or spiritually autonomous; like the person, it has a "moral foundation" and a "metaphysical basis."

The moral measure that governs economics is clearer if we consider economic activity from the perspective of the individual. Morality addresses the human person in his freedom and responsibility, his capacity to choose good or evil. From Plato through Christendom, moral philosophy has taught that the human good requires the subordination of the appetites to reason and moral disposition. This truth holds for the whole of practical life, including the economic sphere. A person who works, saves, invests, buys, sells, and trades his goods with others merely to sate his bodily appetites would be judged immoral and base (not to mention strange). Furthermore, if he were to attempt an abstract explanation and defense of his surely dissolute life on this basis, we would find him incredible (and even stranger).

Acton argues that the same judgment – based on the same moral truth about the human person – ought to inform our evaluation of general economics. If the ultimate justification, the moral premise of the various human relationships that constitute economic life, were mere bodily satisfaction, we would condemn such a system as narrow and low. The basis of our judgment would be the degraded view of the person that it implies. The abstractness of economic analysis does not allow it to suspend concerns about the good of individuals. By grounding economics in the "fulfillment of duties," Acton would establish this science on the moral character of each person – his individual responsibility and his obligation to others. Economics informed by a conception of duty has a solid yet elevated purview; narrow economics, which presents itself as merely a mechanism for the free gratification of appetites, risks censure, even rejection, by morally serious persons.

Ultimately, the vital processes of political economy are not determined by mechanical policies of government. Instead they are governed by the concept of personal excellence, specifically the virtues of "labor, patience, justice, peace, and self-denial." Acton's emphasis on virtue, like his moral anthropology in general, expands the conventional scope of economic discussion. Although labor – the disposition of persons to work – is an essential component of ordinary economic analysis, its place among the virtues named by Acton suggests a greater significance. These virtues, which Acton calls the "mainsprings of economic production," do not obviously concern the material object to be produced; patience, justice, peace, and self-denial primarily address the *subject* of economic activity, the human person. As virtues, they are dispositions of the soul, signs of moral excellence, and good in themselves. The exercise of virtue testifies to the person's transcendent dignity, to his spiritual governance of his material, bodily nature. Acton's anthropological economics also addresses another human duality – each person's individual and social existence. The economic virtues are both interior dispositions, which address the person in his spiritual quietude and self-mastery, and exterior habits, which provide the principles for all social life. Individuals' moral dispositions, rather than programs for the process of production, are the engine driving the production of goods.

A virtue-based conception of economics is, we recognize, useful; for this reason, it may be incorporated easily into conventional economics. Those who are industrious, patient, just, and temperate contribute mightily to the creation of wealth and to a stable, orderly, and fair arrangement of exchange. Yet, in his own day Acton was a critic of what he called "Benthamite systems" – utilitarian economics that focused on mechanical means to the neglect of moral ends. Moral obtuseness remains a limitation of many contemporary economic theories about the operations of the free market. In contrast, the centrality of virtue in Acton's economics precisely illustrates the priority of moral individuals, not abstract systems, in the study of this important human activity. The human good and the moral responsibility of each person are naturally preeminent in every process in which people participate.

Acton's intention to dignify economics in accordance with human dignity leads him to speak of the "metaphysical" foundation for economic activity. As in all things, it is Providence. Matthew 6:33 contains Christ's instruction to persons in their efforts to supply their wordly needs: "Seek ye first the kingdom of God and His justice and all these [necessary] things shall be added to you." This implies, in one aspect, a comprehensive teaching for social life. For each person to aspire to the justice of God is for each to hold virtue – in the forms of fairness and moderation, charity and mercy – as the guiding principle for the treatment of others. Again, conventional economics would surely welcome the practical consequence of this Christian teaching – a system of steady production and equitable exchange. Yet Acton calls on economics to comprehend the greater import of this passage, and, indeed the whole of the sixth chapter of Matthew: the priority of an individual's spiritual and moral calling over his bodily needs and the effort to satisfy them. A person's sustenance will follow from his faith in God and the fulfillment of his moral obligations, Christianity teaches. But the recognition that behind acts of faith and morality is each person's spiritual longing for the good – for God – is the greater, metaphysical truth that Acton addresses to economics.

God's governance of the earth and His plan of redemption calls for each person's participation in an active, moral way. Salvation history may be viewed, e.g. by Augustine, as a sweeping and complex process that embraces all humanity. Yet the Gospels, in particular the sixth chapter of Matthew, testify that the faith and hope, the moral life of each person, is a crucial event in the system of salvation. Acton argues that this supreme insight of theological anthropology reveals practical life as a personal, ethical response to God's calling. Economics, then, is not "mere" economics – simply a system to meet bodily needs or to satisfy bodily desires. It is a great part of each person's active life with others, and thus a reflection of his moral character and, ultimately, his spiritual calling.

In declaring a moral and metaphysical basis for economics, Acton argues that economics ought to be *true* – that is, it must fully comprehend its subject. Acton's statement affirms that the comprehensive account of the human person is contained in Christian revelation – each person is a free but fallen being called to seek God's redemption. Every study of human activity in this life, therefore, including economics, is most truly described as "a *verification* of the promise" made by Christ in Matthew 6:33. God's pledge of provision and salvation must be accomplished by each person in conjunction with God. That accomplishment is through our conscious moral decisions in all spheres of life, Acton suggests. Economic work, like the rest of practical life, is an opportunity and a responsibility for all of us personally and freely to "seek the kingdom of God and His justice." The moral concern that each person brings to his work in the economic sphere is evidence of his dignity and spiritual calling. A study of economics that grasps not only the complex process of free exchange but also each person's fundamental moral concern may be considered a comprehensively true science of economics.

The social teaching of the Catholic Church over the last century has confirmed and developed Acton's humane economics. Pope Leo XIII's 1891 encyclical, *Rerum Novarum*, began the critique of modern economic systems – both capitalism and socialism – from the perspective of the dignity and moral standing of the human person. In two contemporary encyclicals, Pope John Paul II has drawn out the economic teaching of Rerum Novarum in its theological and anthropological depth. *Laborem Exercens* and *Centesimus Annus* are two particularly important contributions to the growing movement to delineate the moral and metaphysical foundations of economic activity.

In *Laborem Exercens*, John Paul speaks to the moral importance of economics through an analysis of the phenomenon of human work. Both Scripture and the diverse social sciences testify that "work is a fundamental dimension of man's existence on earth."[1] Labor characterizes persons not only in their material being – that is, the work that is necessary for subsistence. As John Paul argues, work is also a calling of the highest order. It is a person's practical response to God's command to subdue the earth and have dominion over it, using all the intellectual and moral faculties of a being created in the image of God. Work, then, is discussed in the broadest and most fundamental context in *Laborem Exercens* by focusing on the subject of work, the human person.

Like Acton, John Paul argues that moral reality is the most important and fundamental aspect of any survey of work or economics. Work itself is measured in terms of its utility and efficiency in the larger economic process. However, the value of the worker is that he is "a conscious and free subject" who is capable of "acting in a planned and rational way" and has "a tendency to self-realization."[2] In his criticism of mechanistic or process-centered economics for the moral indifference they imply, Acton affirms that the individual human being, in his essential freedom and obligation, is the fundamental reality of economic activity. Similarly, *Laborem Exercens* calls attention to "the error of economism," which places "the spiritual and the personal" beneath the "material reality" of economic events or of work itself.[3] John Paul recalls to economic study the importance of the human person in declaring that "work is 'for man' and not man 'for work.'"[4]

John Paul argues that the moral content of economic effort – the

good that it represents – addresses human nature in its individual and
social dimensions. Work is good for persons in that, as each freely and
responsibly invests himself in his labor and the material world around
him, work "expresses [his] dignity and increases it."[5] Like Acton, John
Paul focuses on the value of industriousness as "a moral habit . . . something whereby man becomes good as man."[6] Work is also the foundation of family life, and is, therefore, a social good for persons. The
material provision for one's family that comes in most cases by labor-
ing certainly attests to the moral importance of one's work. More sig-
nificantly, though, the subsistence that work provides makes possible
"the whole process of education in the family."[7] Education of children
in the good exercise of their human freedom and talents is itself work,
calling for the utmost personal investment by parents. In an affirmation
of a central tenet of the Church's social teaching, John Paul argues that
the family is the moral association that prepares persons to participate
responsibly in greater human societies. The morality of work embraces
the human good in the practice of familial, societal, and economic relationships.

Centesimus Annus reiterates John Paul's concern for humane economics as part of the Church's broader social teaching. The context of
the encyclical is the sweeping political, technological, and economic
changes in recent years – the "New Things of Today." Yet the foundational truth that informs John Paul's evaluation of socialist political
economies, growing capitalist economies, and advanced consumer
societies is the freedom, dignity, and spiritual vocation of the human
person. The real failure of socialism illustrates the profoundly limited
and false anthropology on which it is based. Socialism represents one
extreme of the process-driven economics that Acton and John Paul
criticize. Socialism treats the individual person merely as "a molecule
within the social organism"; as a consequence, the good of each person
is "completely subordinated to the functioning of the socio-economic
mechanism."[8]

Although the anthropological narrowness of socialism deeply
offends the dignity and responsibility of persons, capitalism and con-
sumerism may also neglect their moral character; the practical foundation of these systems may appear to be merely "the satisfaction of

appetite," in Acton's phrase. The basic human freedom to provide for oneself by one's efforts, which capitalism affirms, is central to the morality of work. Furthermore, John Paul declares in *Centesimus Annus* that the free market is "the most efficient instrument" for employing resources and meeting human needs on the scale of nations.[9] However, the danger of all utilitarian views of economics, even if they affirm a practical aspect of freedom, is the promotion of bodily needs or desires to the exclusion of moral and spiritual goods. There are many true human needs that cannot be met through the free market, and many artificial, unhealthy desires that can be supplied by a morally indifferent market.[10] The corrective to the practical materialism that tragically recurs in economics is a morally vigorous culture that educates both citizens and officials on the principled stewardship of political economy. Although John Paul admits that the Church has no specific economic models to offer, this culture, spearheaded by the Church, still contributes the true conception of the human person and of the common good.[11] The sum of this fundamental teaching is that each person is a free and morally responsible individual, capable of conscious decisions in every sphere of his practical life, and called to live in spiritual communion with his neighbors and with God.

For both Acton and John Paul, the effort to inform economics testifies that the truth about the human person is comprehensive truth. In his obligations and his vocation to God, the person has a "moral foundation" and "metaphysical basis." What is true for persons as individuals holds for them in organized society. The moral and spiritual reality of the person provides a unity, order, and purpose for the different spheres of human activity that are otherwise autonomous. Correctly understood, economics does not contradict but reflects the truth about the human person, a truth contained in Christian revelation. The person is the true fulfillment of economic processes, while God is the fulfillment of the human person. We understand, then, Acton's purpose in concluding his statement on political economy with a promise from the Gospel. The kingdom of God and its justice are both the reality and the hope of each person in all his work on earth.

Notes

1. John Paul II, Encyclical Letter *Laborem Exercens* (September 14, 1981) (Boston: St. Paul Books and Media), 11.

2. Ibid., 15–16.

3. Ibid., 32.

4. Ibid., 17.

5. Ibid., 23.

6. Idem.

7. Ibid., 24.

8. John Paul II, Encyclical Letter *Centesimus Annus* (May 1, 1991) (Boston: St. Paul Books and Media) 20.

9. Ibid., 49.

10. Ibid., 49, 53.

11. Ibid., 60.

Judges

Albert Beck is a Doctoral Fellow at the J. M. Dawson Institute of Church-State studies at Baylor University.

J. Michael Beers, a Roman Catholic priest, is an Associate Professor of Patristic Theology at Mount Saint Mary's Seminary in Emmitsburg, Maryland.

Leonard P. Liggio is Executive Vice-President of the Atlas Economic Research Foundation, Treasurer of the Mont Pelerin Society, Distinguished Senior Scholar at the Institute for Humane Studies, and Research Professor in the Law School at George Mason University. He was formerly President of the Institute for Humane Studies and the Philadelphia Society.

Jennifer Roback Morse is a Senior Fellow of the Acton Institute. She has been on the economics faculties at Yale University and George Mason University. She has written on economics and ethics and on the economics of race relations. She is currently Research Fellow at the Hoover Institution at Stanford.

Edmund Opitz is a Congregational minister. He is a contributing editor of *The Freeman,* the monthly journal of The Foundation for Economic Education, and is a widely published author.

Robert A. Sirico is a Roman Catholic priest and President of the Acton Institute for the Study of Religion and Liberty.

Jeffrey Tucker is Director of Research for the Ludwig von Mises Institute at Auburn University, Auburn, Alabama. He is editor of *The Free Market*, associate editor of *The Austrian Economics Newsletter*, general editor of *Essays in Political Economy*, and assistant director of the annual Austrian Scholars Conference.

Harry C. Veryser is currently the Chairman of the Department of Economics and Finance at Walsh College in Troy, Michigan. In addition, he is Chairman of the Board of Directors of Stampings, Inc., and secretary of Perch Research, International. He has served on the faculties of Northwood Institute, Hillsdale College, Saint Mary's College, and the University of Detroit. Mr. Veryser is the Chairman of the American Council on Economics and Society, a senior member of the Society of Manufacturing Engineers, and a member of the Philadelphia Society.

Authors

Joshua P. Hochschild received his B.A. in 1994 from Yale University, where he majored in philosophy. He is currently pursuing doctoral research in medieval logic and metaphysics at the University of Notre Dame. Upon graduation, he hopes to teach.

Zachary R. Calo is a doctoral candidate in American history at the University of Pennsylvania. He is a Phi Beta Kappa graduate of Johns Hopkins University, having received B.A. and M.A. degrees in history in 1997. His M.A. thesis analyzed the response to poverty in eighteenth-century Maryland. With interests in Christian theological and social ethics, as well as public policy, Mr. Calo is beginning a dissertation which examines twentieth-century American Catholic thought about capitalism, poverty, and liberalism. Upon completing doctoral work in history, he plans to pursue additional studies in law and theology.

Jonathan Barlow, born in Picayune, Mississippi, received B.A. degrees in both philosophy and political science from Mississippi State University. He will graduate in May 1999 from Covenant Theological Seminary in St. Louis, Missouri, with a Master of Divinity degree. He plans to pursue a Ph.D. in theology following seminary education with an eye toward teaching theology at the university or seminary level. His theological interests include biblical and systematic theology as well as prolegomena and ethics. He also has strong interests in philosophy of religion, philosophy of science, and epistemology. Jonathan is a member of the Presbyterian Church in America (PCA), and he frequently teaches adult Sunday school classes. He has a wife, Ann, and two young children, James and Nathan.

Michael Black is currently in his third year of theology at Mount Saint Mary's Seminary in Emmitsburg, Maryland, where he is studying towards ordination to the Catholic priesthood. He graduated from Northwestern University in 1992 with a B.A. in American history and hopes to receive M.A. degrees in divinity and morals upon completing his seminary studies. He looks forward to serving the diocese of Rockford, Illinois, as a parish priest.

Sean Mattie graduated from Middlebury College in 1991 with a B.A. in Political Science. After Middlebury, he earned an M.A. in Political Science, with an emphasis on political philosophy, at Boston College in 1993. He entered the Institute of Philosophic Studies, the doctoral program at the University of Dallas, with a concentration in Politics. His studies in theology and political philosophy at the University of Dallas were advanced by his participation in the 1997 Institute on the Free Society, held in Krakow, Poland. He is currently writing a dissertation on American constitutional law and hopes eventually to teach college or to conduct research at a public policy institute.

James V. Schall, S.J., is Professor of Government at Georgetown University. He is the author of several books, including *At the Limits of Political Philosophy: From "Brilliant Errors" to Things of Uncommon Importance; Reason, Revelation, and the Foundations of Political Philosophy;* and, most recently, *Jacques Maritain: The Philosopher in Society.*

The Acton Institute

Founded in April 1990, the Acton Institute for the Study of Religion and Liberty is named in honor of John Emerich Edward Dalberg Acton, first Baron Acton of Aldenham (1834–1902), the historian of freedom. The mission of the Institute is to promote a society that embraces civil liberties and free-market economics. To that end, the Institute seeks to stimulate dialogue among religious, business, and scholarly communities. The Institute seeks to familiarize those communities, particularly students and seminarians, with the ethical foundations of political liberty and free-market economics. It also serves as a clearinghouse of ideas for entrepreneurs interested in the ethical dimensions of their vital economic and commercial activities.

Described as "the magistrate of history," Lord Acton was one of the great personalities of the nineteenth century and is universally considered to be one of the most learned Englishmen of his time. He made the history of liberty his life's work; indeed, he considered political liberty the essential condition and guardian of religious liberty.

The Institute seeks to advance the cause of liberty by working with religious leaders and business professionals to promote the moral and economic dimensions of freedom. Lord Acton understood that liberty is "the delicate fruit of a mature civilization" and that in every age the progress of religious, economic, and political liberty is challenged, even threatened, by its adversaries. Likewise, in our own age, liberty is under constant siege. It is our hope that by demonstrating the compatibility of religion, liberty, and free economic activity, religious leaders and entrepreneurs can forge an alliance that will serve to foster and secure a free and virtuous society.